Father's Sayings

>-<

by Eugene Peterson

The contents of this work, including, but not limited to, the accuracy of events, people, and places depicted; opinions expressed; permission to use previously published materials included; and any advice given or actions advocated are solely the responsibility of the author, who assumes all liability for said work and indemnifies the publisher against any claims stemming from publication of the work.

All Rights Reserved
Copyright © 2021 by Eugene Peterson

No part of this book may be reproduced or transmitted, downloaded, distributed, reverse engineered, or stored in or introduced into any information storage and retrieval system, in any form or by any means, including photocopying and recording, whether electronic or mechanical, now known or hereinafter invented without permission in writing from the publisher.

Dorrance Publishing Co
585 Alpha Drive
Suite 103
Pittsburgh, PA 15238
Visit our website at *www.dorrancebookstore.com*

ISBN: 978-1-6480-4797-8
eISBN: 978-1-6480-4476-2

Father's Sayings

1.
Use your mind, body, and soul.

2.
God first, and everything will follow.

3.
No problem is bigger than you.

4.
Respect others as you wish to be respected.

5.
Love conquers evil.

6.
Left or right; no in between.

7.
Every problem is minute.

8.
Watch out for pretty tony.

9.
Always be a leader, not a follower.

10.
Money is the root to all evil.

11.
Respect God, not money.

12.
You can't pick family, but you can pick friends.

13.
If you don't listen, you don't learn.

14.
You're always a student and a teacher for life.

15.
Your faith will set you free.

16.
Thank God for what you have and not what you want.

17.
Older people are wiser; respect and listen.

18.
The wind is blowing, but you can't see it.

19.
Your mind is a muscle. Make sure you use it.

20.
Love yourself, or no one will.

21.
First God, yourself, family, and friends.

22.
Do it today, not tomorrow.

23.
Time does not wait.

24.
Yesterday is gone; today is yours.

25.
It doesn't cost nothing to be nice.

26.
There are many words in the dictionary; learn them.

27.
Think before you talk.

28.
Make time for God and a prayer.

29.
Use your third eye.

30.
You and God have your own private relation.

31.
The path to God is yours.

32.
Good food, Good meat, Good God, let's eat.

33.
Don't let your mind get bigger than your heart.

34.
Make today benefit you tomorrow.

35.
Learn to forgive and move on.

36.
Jesus is your answer.

37.
Your spirit is your Armor.

38.
Your heart is your temple.

39.
If you lie you have to lie again.
The truth would set you free.

40.
The first school is home.

41.
Father is the King of his castle,
and the wife is the Queen.

42.
Responsibility brings maturity.

43.
Respect the rules, and follow them.

44.
If your lips are moving, you're not listening.

45.
Brush your teeth, or don't open your mouth.

46.
Kill them with your kindness.

47.
Go ask your mother.

48.
Do as I say, not as I do.

49.
Money doesn't grow on trees.

50.
A little dirt won't hurt you.

51.
Chew with your mouth closed.

52.
Eat your vegetables.

53.
Listen, or you will be disciplined.

54.
Love and hate is always together.

55.
There's a thin line between love and hate.

56.

It's always three stories for the truth.

57.

Don't worry; it will fit you later.

58.

Father's nightmare, your first won't be your last.

59.

Tel-lie-vision.

60.

Patience is always necessary.

61.

You can't see the future, but you can make your future.

62.
I will give you a hand, but don't take my arm.

63.
I don't have to give you my time, but I am here.

64.
My house is yours forever

65.
I am your father forever; you can't divorce me.

66.
God is the Judge, not you.

67.
If you give, do it with your heart and soul.

68.
To be good is harder than to be bad.

69.
Treasure your family and friends
because the time will end.

70.
Life is short; make something out of it.

71.
The rule of my house is poetic justice.

72.
Do not speak when Dad's speaking

73.
You want to know what's wrong, look in the mirror.

74.
I cannot take your test.

75.
Don't worry; trust God.

76.
Do not waste your youth. You will get older.

77.
Go for your goals. I can't.

78.
Do not be scared of love;
it will make you stronger.

79.
The only one you should fear is God.

80.
Do not be a couch potato; enjoy the world.

81.
Your first impressions are usually right.

82.
Learn how to take criticism for your benefit.

83.
Money can come and go real fast.

84.
Watch what you eat, or nobody will watch you.

85.
My sayings are from my heart and soul.

86.
Peace with God will save you.

87.
Keep your faith. God's with you.

88.
If you practice routinely what you want,
it will be automatic.

89.
Try not to fool yourself; you will go crazy.

90.
You have the chance to make it right.

91.
Hobbies, laughter, and joy make your life better.

92.
You can always repent;
God will always forgive you.

93.
Dreams and needs can always happen.

94.
Always try to achieve your first priority.

95.
God will answer, but you must call.

96.
You are never alone; he's always there, so are we.

97.
Don't be scared, Dad's here.

98.
There is no exception to the rule: everybody gets fooled.

99.
You must realize pity is self-destruction.

100.
Keep your guard up. The devil is always there.

101.
My love is always with you.

102.
Being ungrateful is selfishness.

103.
Don't be scared of love; it might not be there later.

104.
Do it now; later might not be available.

105.
You are your problem.

106.
Make yourself likable to you.

107.
Treasure your blessings, not your needs.

108.
Kid's think with their hearts, not their minds.

109.
Headbone is connected to the neckbone;
you cannot pull it apart.

110.
Watch what you say, or you will regret it later.

111.
You will be an example of yourself, family, and friends.

112.
Bad times, you can always see good out of it.

113.
Your spirit will always guide you.

114.
Thank God every day for your life.

115.
If you second guess it, it's usually wrong.

116.
Be proud of yourself, who and what you are,
it will bring happiness.

117.
Too much sugar turns sour.

118.
Making decisions is a part of life

119.
Life is four quarters;
don't let the first mess up the second.

120.
Mind over matter, if you matter.

121.
It's so easy, it's hard.

122.
Always try to like what you see in the mirror.

123.
Doubting yourself will make it harder.

124.
You have so much inside, but you have to pull it out.

125.
In your prayers, ask for guidance,
strength, protections, and thank Him.

126.
Appreciate what you give or receive.
It will make you happy.

127.
Unfortunately, happiness and sadness
always come together.

128.
Your time is valuable and short
to do what you want to do.

129.
God makes it right; the devil makes it left.

130.
Your feet grow first; hope the rest grow with them.

131.
Each step can make it better or worse.

132.
God knows what you think, say, and do before you.

133.
I want your life to be better than mine.

134.
Teaching what I have is my duty.

135.
Loving you is my blessing.

136.
Committing and sharing is God's law.

137.
Look deep inside; it turns into your spirit.

138.
Walk before you run; tripping can be painful.

139.
Greediness and selfishness should not be on your resume.

140.
Wanting and having are two different subjects.

141.
It's not what you say, it's what you do.

142.
Only you can make me love you.

143.
Your mind can change my mind.

144.
If you prepare for it, you will succeed.

145.
If you study, you won't fail.

146.
Negative thinking brings nothing but anger.

147.
Caring and sharing makes the room lighter.

148.
Put the light on; you can't see.

149.
You're using half your brain.

150.
Making a difference makes you feel better.

151.
Jealousy is selfishness.

152.
Having love is a blessing.

153.
Use your brain; it will keep you out of trouble.

154.
Being mean doesn't help.

155.
You are smarter than you think.

156.
Stop cheating yourself.

157.
Work now, play later.

158.
If you don't have it, you can't miss it.

159.
Flowers grow only when you water them.

160.
Memories are forever.

161.
Feelings hurt it's painful.

162.
Be humble and appreciate.

163.
No one owes you anything.

164.
Do not be cripple; do it yourself.

165.
What you see is not what you have,
but what you can get.

166.
You cannot see Him, but God is here.

167.
If you don't do it, it's your loss.

168.
If you have it, share it. Be nice.

169.
No one can copyright you; you're by yourself.

170.
Respect your teacher. He can bring a better tomorrow.

171.
Your words are vital. Use them wisely.

172.
Read the whole book, not one page.

173.
Having love and giving love is a blessing.

174.
Loyalty will take you a long way.

175.
Don't ignore the signs you see.

176.
Life is short, and death is fast.

177.
You can fool everybody but God.

178.
You are accountable for what you say and do.

179.
Holidays are for giving love.

180.
Listen to your unconscious and spiritual mind;
it will show you the right way.

181.
Eat right, think right, go right.

182.
Don't let your dreams and goals fade away.

183.
If you have a puppy, you feed it, clean it, and train it.

184.
If you don't understand, ask again.

185.
Your life should be like a ladder, to go higher.

186.

Always practice what you preach.

187.

You learn to earn.

188.

If you have or haven't,
it doesn't characterize who you are.

189.

If you hesitate, it's usually too late.

190.

When you're right, prove it;
when you're wrong, accept it.

191.
Life can be bitter or sweet. It's up to you.

192.
The choices you make can help or destroy you.

193.
Always remember, there's light at the end of the tunnel.

194.
If you fake it, you're hurting yourself.

195.
If you can see it, show it. Make God happy.

196.
Make sure you read and learn something new every day.

197.
If you don't try, you will not succeed.

198.
Do not forget the beauty around you.

199.
Whether it's bad or good, your faith is always needed.

200.
Know God, live with God; it's the only right way.

CPSIA information can be obtained
at www.ICGtesting.com
Printed in the USA
BVHW050836260521
608176BV00001B/7